WEEKLY **WR** READER®
EARLY LEARNING LIBRARY

Where People Work

What Happens at a

Bike Shop?

by Kathleen Pohl

Reading consultant: Susan Nations, M.Ed., author/literacy coach/consultant in literacy development

Please visit our web site at: www.garethstevens.com
For a free color catalog describing Weekly Reader® Early Learning Library's list
of high-quality books, call 1-877-445-5824 (USA) or 1-800-387-3178 (Canada).
Weekly Reader® Early Learning Library's fax: (414) 336-0164.

Library of Congress Cataloging-in-Publication Data

Pohl, Kathleen.
   What happens at a bike shop? / by Kathleen Pohl.
      p. cm. — (Where people work)
   Includes bibliographical references and index.
   ISBN-10: 0-8368-6885-4 — ISBN-13: 978-0-8368-6885-2 (lib. bdg.)
   ISBN-10: 0-8368-6892-7 — ISBN-13: 978-0-8368-6892-0 (softcover)
   1. Bicycles—Juvenile literature.   2. Bicycle stores—Juvenile literature.
I. Title.   II. Series: Pohl, Kathleen. Where people work.
   TL412.P65   2007
   381'.456292272—dc22   2006007673

This edition first published in 2007 by
Weekly Reader® Early Learning Library
A Member of the WRC Media Family of Companies
330 West Olive Street, Suite 100
Milwaukee, Wisconsin 53212 USA

Managing editor: Dorothy L. Gibbs
Art direction: Tammy West
Cover design and page layout: Scott M. Krall
Picture research: Diane Laska-Swanke and Kathleen Pohl
Photographer: Jack Long

Acknowledgments: The publisher thanks Dominique and Sigrunn Mosley and John Jensen
for modeling in this book. Special thanks to John Jensen, of Johnson's Cycle & Fitness, for
his expert consulting and the use of his shop's facilities.

Printed in the United States of America

1 2 3 4 5 6 7 8 9 10 09 08 07 06

Hi, Kids!

I'm Buddy, your Weekly Reader® pal. Have you ever visited a bike shop? I'm here to show and tell what happens at a bike shop. So, come on. Turn the page and read along!

Dominic wants to buy a bike. This bike shop has lots of them, in all sizes and colors!

Some bikes are red. Some are blue. Some have three wheels. Some have two.

Mr. Jensen owns the bike shop. He is helping Dominic choose a bike. Dominic's new bike must be just the right size for him.

He can try out some bikes right in Mr. Jensen's shop. Whee! Look out, Dominic!

Mr. Jensen has a workshop in the back of his store. He has lots of tools in his workshop. He uses the tools to fix broken bikes.

Mr. Jensen also uses his tools on new bikes. New bikes come in pieces. The pieces are packed in boxes.

BRONCO

Mr. Jensen uses tools to put the pieces together. First, he attaches the front wheel. He uses a tool called a **wrench**.

wrench

Next, Mr. Jensen attaches the **pedals**. Then he will attach the seat and the **handlebars**.

pedal

Dominic's bike is ready to ride. Don't forget to wear a safety helmet, Dominic!

Glossary

handlebars — the bar across the front of a bike that has a handle at each end for steering

helmet — a hard hat that keeps the head safe

pedals — the parts of a bike moved by the feet to make the bike go forward

workshop — a place with tools where a person can build or fix things

wrench — a tool used to twist something to make it tight

 For More Information

Books

How Is a Bicycle Made? Angela Royston
   (Heinemann Library)

I Can Ride a Bike. Edana Eckart (Childrens Press)

Look Out! A Story about Safety on Bicycles.
   The Hero Club (series). Cindy Leaney (Rourke)

Web Site

Propelled by Pedals: Choosing a Bike
   library.thinkquest.org/J002670/preferences.htm
   Find out the what, where, and how of buying a bike.

Publisher's note to educators and parents: Our editors have carefully reviewed these Web sites to ensure that they are suitable for children. Many Web sites change frequently, however, and we cannot guarantee that a site's future contents will continue to meet our high standards of quality and educational value. Be advised that children should be closely supervised whenever they access the Internet.

 # Index

About the Author

Kathleen Pohl has written and edited many children's books. Among them are animal tales, rhyming books, retold classics, and the forty-book series *Nature Close-Ups*. She also served for many years as top editor of *Taste of Home* and *Country Woman* magazines. She and her husband, Bruce, live among beautiful Wisconsin woods and share their home with six goats, a llama, and all kinds of wonderful woodland creatures.